The Washington State Growth Management Act: Plain and Simple

Clayton Petree - Jack Petree

A Primer: Washington's Growth Management Act

Washington State's Growth Management Act (GMA) has an impact, every day, on every citizen in Washington State. The Act affects our jobs, it attempts to affect where and how we live, most of the decisions made by, especially, local governments are predicated on provisions of the Act and, to a significant extent, our lives in community have changed over time because of the Act.

Why Are We Required To Plan Under The Act?

In 1990, after a surprisingly brief period of discussion and process, the Washington State Legislature adopted RCW 36.70A; the Growth Management Act (GMA). Explaining the reasoning behind the act the legislature put forward:

RCW 36.70A.010 Legislative findings... What Olympia Intended

"The legislature finds that uncoordinated and unplanned growth, together with a lack of common goals expressing the public's interest in the conservation and the wise use of our lands, pose a threat to the environment, sustainable economic development, and the health, safety, and high quality of life enjoyed by residents of this state. It is in the public interest that citizens, communities, local governments, and the private sector cooperate and coordinate with one another in comprehensive land use planning. Further, the legislature finds that it is in the public interest that economic development programs be shared with communities experiencing insufficient economic growth."

Introduction by the Authors

First, it must be known that this book is not intended to be an exhaustive digest containing an answer to every question about the Washington State Growth Management Act. Rather, it is intended to be a brief and informational introduction to what is often referred to as simply the "GMA" - in as brief a manner as such a large and all encompassing law allows for. Those wishing for a more exhaustive, technical document can find the answer to nearly any question in the State produced, so called "Short Course on Local Planning Resource Guide."

Washington State passed its Growth Management act, "GMA" in 1990 and refined that law in 1991 and later years. One of the principal objectives of Washington's GMA is to direct the vast majority of new development at urban densities into urban growth areas (UGAs). The GMA depends heavily on the use of UGAs to "reduce the inappropriate conversion of undeveloped land into sprawling, low-density development." Urban growth is supposed to be encouraged inside UGAs, while outside UGAs only non-urban growth is supposed to occur.

The Washington State Department of Community Development (now the Department of Commerce) provided the following advice (Easley 1990) with regard to urban growth areas: "Enough land must be included within the urban growth area to provide sufficient land to accommodate projected market demand within the prescribed planning period, with additional land to provide choice. If too little land is included, exorbitant increases in the cost of land and housing and legal challenges and political pressure to prematurely extend the urban growth boundaries may result. On the other hand, designation of too large an area defeats the purposes of encouraging compact development and usually results in excessive and premature capital outlays for services." While the law clearly intends most future growth and population will be directed to locate inside UGAs, planning jurisdictions are also required to provide an opportunity to live, work and play in non-urban areas for those desiring a rural lifestyle. To allow that opportunity, those counties required to plan under GMA are expected to include a "rural" element of their comprehensive plans, thus setting aside some supply of land for rural development, distinct from those lands preserved for agriculture, forestry, or mineral resource extraction. Counties required to plan under GMA provide their own definitions of what is urban and not urban. In rural growth areas, counties are supposed to preserve rural-based economies and traditional rural lifestyles, provide for a variety of rural business opportunities, and assure citizens who want to participate in the rural experience are able to participate (RCW.70A.070(5). While accommodating rural lifestyles, UGAs should be used to develop and implement GMA goals for population growth.

Carrots vs. Stick Approach

At the heart of any successful attempt to manage the location of population growth in a region or county is the answer to the question: "Will new populations accept the lifestyle choices (form and character) offered by planners and decision makers seeking to influence where growth is captured in that region?" The question is especially important in a context where voters have a say. Few would disagree; a growth management effort is more likely to be effective in achieving planning goals aimed at enhancing community if residents are drawn to the places set aside for growth than if citizens must be driven to those places.

In our opinion, Washington's GMA is overtly based on the carrot approach to growth management rather than use of the stick. Citizens are to have choices. Citizens are to be enticed into UGAs, but not forced into them. An adequate, 20 year land supply is viewed to be fundamental to providing that choice under GMA. The assumption is that new populations can be enticed to settle in the "right place" (i.e., within UGAs) if appropriate land supplies and access to urban infrastructure exist. When choice is seriously restricted, especially in terms of land supplies for favored housing types, new populations will refuse to locate in "acceptable" places and will seek out alternatives, as has happened in the past; an issue the legislature sought to address through passage of the GMA.

Above, a healthy mix of jobs, housing types, and amenities allows cities to capture growth.

Washington's Law - How it is Organized

The Revised Code Of Washington (RCW)

"The Revised Code of Washington (RCW) is the compilation of all permanent laws now in force. It is a collection of Session Laws (enacted by the Legislature, and signed by the Governor, or enacted via the initiative process), arranged by topic, with amendments added and repealed laws removed. It does not include temporary laws such as appropriations acts."

RCWs are arranged by Title, Chapter and Section. For example, RCW 36.70A.010, the legislative findings regarding the GMA is:

1. **Title - 36:** Counties
2. **Chapter 70A:** Growth management -- Planning by selected counties and cities.
3. **Section 010:** Legislative findings

The Washington Administrative Code (WAC) Provides Regulations Needed To Implement Law

"Regulations of executive branch agencies are issued by authority of statutes. Like legislation and the Constitution, regulations are a source of primary law in Washington State. The WAC codifies the regulations and arranges them by subject or agency."

WACs are also organized by Title, Chapter and, Section.

WAC Title 365, Chapters 195 and 196 Provide Much Of The Regulatory Support For The GMA

The Origins Of The Growth Management Act

Washington's Growth Management Act (GMA) came into being in 1990 after several years of pressure by environmental activist groups, business interests, academics, political decision makers, the public and, others.

(1) Environmental groups worried about "rampant sprawl" in the countryside away from the cities;

(2) Business interests worried about increasing restrictions on the ability to do business;

(3) Cities and counties worried about the costs of new roads and other public infrastructure needed when growth occurs;

(4) Academics of the time looked to the perceived benefits of growth management in places like Oregon;

(5) Farm groups worried about the impacts of growth on costs and the right to farm;

(6) And most of all…

Regardless of the facts regarding growth, public perception about the value of growth changed dramatically in the second half of the 20th Century. The long prevalent idea that growth was not only a good thing but something necessary to the enhancement of quality of life for all citizens came to be replaced by a feeling that growth, especially population growth, created more negatives than positives.

Uncoordinated And Unplanned Growth

Earth Day 1970 is often considered to be the "birthday" of the modern environmental movement. In the decade following Earth Day many of the present day giants of the environmental protest movement (Greenpeace and others) were founded as Viet Nam war protesters, and those influenced by the war protests, shifted their attention from Viet Nam to a new cause, turned battleground; the environment.

Because most environmental ills were considered to be caused by mankind's impact on the environment, the attention of the environmental movements, especially in Washington State, turned to growth management. As a result:

(1) Cities and counties began to implement comprehensive planning aimed at managing growth within their boundaries;

(2) The emphasis of comprehensive planning turned from an emphasis on economic development to environmental preservation;

(3) Disdain for growth, especially population growth, began to be reflected in local planning efforts;

Myths And Facts

In 1990, Richard Morrill and David C Hodge of the University of Washington's Department of Geography, two of Washington's most respected minds regarding growth management, wrote an essay titled *Myths and Facts About Growth Management*. The paper addressed, "…some of the most popular perceptions about growth, growth management, housing and transportation which are not supported by the best empirical evidence gleaned from existing research." Among other insights the two experts commented that:

"Survey research tells us that many people are indeed worried about traffic congestion, loss of open space and environmental impacts resulting from growth. They are also equally concerned about higher housing costs. A sizable minority would like to prevent growth altogether. Most, however, seem willing to accept some growth but also seek stronger growth management by local governments."

However, the two men warned:

"The relationships between population growth, traffic, mass transit, housing and land economics are extremely complex and not well understood by the general public, their elected officials or even professional planners."

As to the just passed and soon to be amended Washington Growth Management Act (GMA) the two concluded:

"Until we understand the complex dynamics of growth, we are unlikely to reach a consensus for our own future and are likely to be dissatisfied with the long-term results of current planning efforts."

"Planning Becomes Egocentric"

In Washington State, prior to the 1980s, many communities engaged in "comprehensive" planning for the future growth of cities, towns, and counties. Plans tended to be based on "visioning" or "community preferences" regarding the future rather than solid data.

Over time, "planning for growth" and all that might imply morphed into the much more aggressive, "growth management." A public philosophy embracing population and, especially, economic growth shifted into one in which growth was seen as a possible threat to quality of life.

Washington's cities and counties had been engaged in comprehensive community planning for decades and, because it is the nature of local government to respond to local concerns comprehensive plan updates in the 1980s tended to meet two objectives:

(1) Assure to the extent possible that population and other kinds of "undesirable" growth is shifted to other jurisdictions and;
(2) Ensure only "desirable" growth continues in our community.

Comprehensive plans developed as a result of the planning efforts were often treated as politically motivated wish lists, convenient for use in stopping or shifting growth rather than managing inevitable growth.

A Lack Of Common Goals

An ego-centric approach to planning in the '70s and '80s meant that adjoining jurisdictions regularly developed planning approaches that were in opposition to one another's goals and policies.

1. Some jurisdictions focused on a strong economy while rejecting population growth;
2. Some jurisdictions hyper-focused on environmental protection, rejecting all growth as a matter of public policy;
3. Some jurisdictions focused on attracting only certain economic sectors while attempting to reject others;
4. Some jurisdictions, especially smaller cities and counties, retained traditional approaches to planning.

Survival Of The Shiftiest – "We'll Take The Good Growth, You Take The Bad"

Competing goals led to shifts in the economic, geographical, political and, demographic structure of the State.

1. Seattle and Spokane lose significant population in the decades preceding the GMA. Neither city recovered its 1960 population level until the census of 2000.
2. Seattle's policies during the time focus on building jobs. Population growth is considered less acceptable to the city.
3. 1960 – 2000 Seattle gains 267,000 jobs but only sees a 6,650 person increase in population.
4. Spokane County and King County outside of Spokane and Seattle city limits, on the other hand, gain significant population even as their major cities lose population. Most population growth, 1960 – 2000 took place around the two county's major cities.
5. Even Oregon shifted significant growth to Washington. While basking in the glow of academic excitement over the Oregon growth management plan, Oregon's lack of planning regarding its northern boundary meant just across the State border, Washington's Clark County took a population hit. Portland's much touted Urban Growth Boundaries acted as a pressure cooker without a lid; squeezing populations north, across the Columbia River. Between 1960 and 1990 Clark County's population grew by more than 250%.

Growth Management, Acts One and Two

As the last decade of the 20th Century approached, coalitions of citizens were being formed and pressure was beginning to mount on the legislature to "do something, anything" about the perceived negatives of population growth. Not wanting to be left out and fearing either too much new regulation or, too little, representatives of a broad range of business, professional, environmental, farm and forest, and other organizations came to the table to discuss the issues. This bi-partisan process, surprisingly, took under 3 years to occur including a significant update one year after adoption.

1989: Governor Booth Gardner establishes a "Growth Strategies Commission" to research strategies for handling growth throughout the state. The 20 member commission includes representatives from a broad variety of interests.

1989: Speaker of the House Joe King establishes a committee of six House committee chairs charged with producing a draft of a proposed growth management act.

1990: The Growth Management Act (RCW 36.70A) is passed much to the surprise of almost everyone involved in the growth debate. A provision in the Act calls for the Growth Strategies Commission to continue work to refine the Act.

1991: Significant additions to the Act are passed into law. Additions include Growth Management Hearings Boards, a requirement that County Wide Planning Policies be adopted and, others.

The Dream: Sharing The Burdens Of Growth – Sharing The Benefits Of Growth

The Growth Management Act, more commonly known as the "GMA" was designed to be an elegant balance of requirements to plan for managing growth less selfishly in the future even as it allows communities to preserve the best of what they have now.

Growth management is about enhancing the environment, improving the economy, and preserving quality of life for every citizen.

The GMA is about balance

It's About Preserving The Best Of The Old

As We Work To Build Something New

Why the GMA "Makes Us Do It"

Jobs and other economic opportunity, environmental quality and the overall quality of life was, and is, unevenly shared throughout the state. The GMA was passed to provide opportunity for all based on local needs and desires.

The GMA Was Passed To Provide For:

1. Environmental preservation;
2. Economic enhancement;
3. Quality of Life for all;

To Be Achieved By

1. Coordinating growth across jurisdictional lines;
2. Planning for growth using a minimum 20 year timeframe;
3. Utilizing a common set of goals to plan for growth statewide.

http://www.ofm.wa.gov/news/release/2014/140630.asp

Coordinating Growth Across Jurisdictional Lines

An innovation brought about by the GMA is the requirement that approaches to growth must be coordinated across jurisdictional lines. Watersheds, for example, may cross city, county, state and even international boundaries. Coordinating planning across jurisdictional lines allows the concerns and needs of all jurisdictions to be considered as planning for a 20+ year planning horizon is addressed. Cities, counties, and other jurisdictions are required, among other things, to:

1. Develop County-wide planning policies governing growth approaches common to both city and county comprehensive plans - RCW 36.70A.210;
2. Develop comprehensive plans that are coordinated and consistent with the plans of adjoining jurisdictions. Counties must coordinate with cities and cities must coordinate with counties. Counties must also coordinate with adjoining counties – RCW 36.70A.100;
3. Counties and cities must review comprehensive plans regularly to assure consistency and adequacy with one another. RCW 36.70A.130;
4. Counties and cities must plan together to assure sufficient land capacity for development – RCW 36.70A.115.

In general, comprehensive plans and the development regulations needed to implement them must not only be internally consistent but consistent with those of adjoining or overlapping jurisdictions as well.

Literally hundreds of local, regional and statewide jurisdictions interact and must be accounted for as cities and counties plan for future growth.

Puget Sound Regional Council Planning Map

Central Puget Sound Watersheds

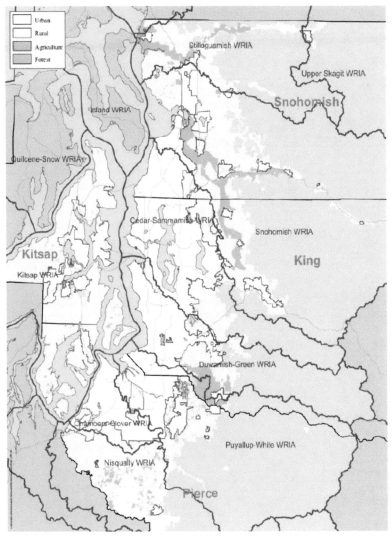

The Law Does Not Allow Us To "Just Say No" To Growth

1. Not one word can be found in the GMA regarding reducing or stopping growth;
2. Nor does the GMA specifically encourage growth;
3. The GMA does require that we plan for expected growth;
4. The title of the act explains the legislation's purpose. We are dealing with the Growth **Management** Act.

And Most Important!

To the chagrin of many, Comprehensive Plans and other planning instruments developed under the auspices of the GMA **are actually required to be utilized to manage growth!**

A serious issue confounding efforts to achieve some of the goals of the Growth Management Act during the Act's first quarter century of existence has been resistance by cities and counties to the requirement that Comprehensive Plans *must be implemented*. The Act changed planning documents from wistfully dreamy plans that could or should be followed into directive, authoritative documents that *shall* be implemented.

An equal problem has been an entire generation of planners, attorneys, and, others charged with overseeing implementation of the Comprehensive Plans meant to direct jurisdiction's responses to growth were educated in a pre-growth management era; when comprehensive plans and fairy tales had much the same impact on actual growth in a community.

All that has meant enforcement of the Act's provisions has been uneven and, worse, Comprehensive Planning has been susceptible to manipulation as highly organized and well-funded activist groups have dominated the quasi-judicial dispute resolution process established by the GMA.

Hearings Boards Provide For Unique Public Oversight...
Sometimes

The dispute resolution process established by GMA first involves appeal to an appointed Growth Management Hearings Board, a board with quasi-judicial powers. One of the reasons the legislature added the Hearings Board concept to the act is to make the appeal process available, at fairly low cost, to ordinary citizens who may appear "*pro se*" or, on their own behalf. However:

1. Hearings Board decisions can be appealed to the courts but only at *tremendous* expense. Most appellants, especially those appealing *pro se* cannot afford the cost of an appeal to a court;.
2. Appeals aren't as costly to the jurisdictions involved in the appeal as is sometimes claimed because often already hired staff defends the jurisdiction so jurisdictions have found simply digging in their heels and resisting citizen appeals can make even the best justified appeals simply go away;
3. Hearings Boards are routinely overruled by the courts on appeal, even earning what amounts to a scolding in some recent cases;
4. A method allowing inexpensive appeals to *pro se* challenges would likely lead to better growth management decisions and approaches.

Planning For At Least 20 Years Of Growth

Eighteen counties were mandated to plan when the GMA was adopted in 1990. In addition, eleven other counties opted to place themselves under the requirements of the GMA. *All of the state's counties must plan for critical areas and resource lands.*

Growth Management Act – County Map

Mandated to Plan, Opting to Plan, and Planning Only for Critical Areas and Resource Lands

Counties Mandated to Plan	
Chelan (1990)	Mason (1990)*
Clallam (1990)	Pierce (1990)
Clark (1990)	San Juan (1990)*
Grant (1992)	Skagit (1990)
Island (1990)	Snohomish (1990)
Jefferson (1990)*	Spokane (1993)
King (1990)	Thurston (1990)
Kitsap (1990)	Whatcom (1990)
Lewis (1994)	Yakima (1990)

Counties Opting to Plan	
Benton (1990)	Kittitas (1990)
Columbia (1991)	Pacific (1990)
Douglas (1990)	Pend Oreille (1990)
Ferry (1990)	Stevens (1993)
Franklin (1990)	Walla Walla (1990)
Garfield (1991)	

Counties Planning Only for Critical Areas and Resource Lands	
Adams	Lincoln
Asotin	Okanogan
Cowlitz	Skamania**
Grays Harbor	Wahkiakum
Klickitat	Whitman

*   Did not exercise ability to opt-out of full GMA planning
** Exercised ability to opt-out of full GMA planning

Department of Commerce
Innovation is in our nature.

Growth Management Services

1011 Plum Street SE
P.O. Box 42525
Olympia, WA 98504-2525
(360) 725-3066

November 2013

A Twenty Year, Non-Rolling Horizon Is Meant To Provide Certainty

At the heart of the GMA is a requirement that cities and counties create Comprehensive Plans capable of accommodating growth projected for the 20 years succeeding the creation of the plan.

1. The state Office of Financial Management (OFM) is required to estimate the most likely future population for the state's counties, with a range of uncertainty represented by a maximum and minimum;
2. Counties, in conjunction with their cities, use the OFM projection range to allocate population and employment growth to the county's cities, non city areas and, in some counties, to unincorporated Urban Growth Areas;
3. The cities and county must create Comprehensive Plans showing how allocated growth can be accommodated over the 20 years being planned for.

Comprehensive planning for an extended timeframe is intended to allow, especially, adequate infrastructure planning based on where growth is planned to take place. Schools can be built near where students are likely to live, roads adequate to handle projected traffic can be built where traffic is likely, sewer and water systems adequately sized can be built where housing, commerce and other activities are likely to be sited. Benefits are presumed to include:

1. Growth takes place in areas where public policy decisions have established a preference for growth;
2. Infrastructure can be properly sized and located;

3. Investors in a community can make decisions based on an established plan; certainty is important when investing in a community.

While plans are updated periodically, with staggered 7 and 10 year timeframes, there is what is referred to as a non-rolling 20 year timeframe in which public services will be available to develop designated urban land to urban densities. The hearings boards of the 1990s referenced this requirement in many cases, but makes the concept crystal clear in this excerpt from the Hearings board digest:
"Designation of a traditional UGA generally establishes certainty that: 1) the development of the land within it will be urban in nature; 2) this urban land will ultimately be provided with adequate urban facilities and services within the planning horizon; and 3) the land will ultimately be developed at urban densities and intensities. [Johnson II, 97-3-0002, FDO, at 10.]"

Coordinated and Planned Growth Based On Common Goals

The GMA addresses fourteen emphasis points, called "Planning Goals." Cities and counties must address the GMA's planning goals as those jurisdictions create local plans. Jurisdictions are supposed to, but don't always, show how each of the goals is met as comprehensive planning takes place (RCW 36.70A.020). **Urban growth:** Encourage development in urban areas where adequate public facilities and services exist or can be provided in an efficient manner.

GMA planning goals are:

1. **Urban growth:** Encourage development in urban areas where adequate public facilities and services exist or can be provided in an efficient manner.

2. **Reduce sprawl:** Reduce the inappropriate conversion of undeveloped land into sprawling, low-density development.

3. **Transportation:** Encourage efficient multimodal transportation systems that are based on regional priorities and coordinated with county and city comprehensive plans.

4. **Housing:** Encourage the availability of affordable housing to all economic segments of the population of this state, promote a variety of residential densities and housing types, and encourage preservation of existing housing stock.

5. **Economic development:** Encourage economic development throughout the state that is consistent with adopted comprehensive plans, promote economic

opportunity for all citizens of this state, especially for unemployed and for disadvantaged persons, promote the retention and expansion of existing businesses and recruitment of new businesses, recognize regional differences impacting economic development opportunities, and encourage growth in areas experiencing insufficient economic growth, all within the capacities of the state's natural resources, public services, and public facilities.

6. **Property rights:** Private property shall not be taken for public use without just compensation having been made. The property rights of landowners shall be protected from arbitrary and discriminatory actions.

7. **Permits:** Applications for both state and local government permits should be processed in a timely and fair manner to ensure predictability.

8. **Natural resource industries:** Maintain and enhance natural resource-based industries, including productive timber, agricultural, and fisheries industries. Encourage the conservation of productive forest lands and productive agricultural lands, and discourage incompatible uses.

9. **Open space and recreation:** Retain open space, enhance recreational opportunities, conserve fish and wildlife habitat, increase access to natural resource lands and water, and develop parks and recreation facilities.

10. **Environment:** Protect the environment and enhance the state's high quality of life, including air and water quality, and the availability of water.

11. **Citizen participation and coordination:** Encourage the involvement of citizens in the planning process and ensure coordination between communities and jurisdictions to reconcile conflicts.

12. **Public facilities and services:** Ensure that those public facilities and services necessary to support development shall be adequate to serve the development at the time the development is available for occupancy and use without decreasing current service levels below locally established minimum standards.

13. **Historic preservation:** Identify and encourage the preservation of lands, sites, and structures, that have historical or archaeological significance.

14. **Shoreline Management Act:** The goals and policies of the shoreline management act were added as a GMA goal in 1995.

Fourteen Goals – Each Is To Be Equally Important

Washington's GMA, in contrast to Oregon's, emphasizes local control when it comes to planning. While GMA does not prioritize the 14 goals for growth management established by the Act, in practice:

1. While local jurisdiction must show how they intend to assure GMA goals are met, those same jurisdictions can, and do, emphasize some goals over others;
2. Some goals are intrinsically called out as having more importance through the use of words like "shall," and "ensure," in setting out parameters that may not be violated, or ignored, by local jurisdictions;
3. The Act itself also assures some goals are complied with by requiring certain kinds of actions dealing directly with some of the goals of the Act.
4. Large amount of local discretion is allowed so long as the overarching goals are achieved.
5. Local goals above and beyond those called out in the Act may be developed but they may not conflict with the achievement of "Common Goals" set out to benefit all.

The Meat Of The GMA – A Tough Nut To Crack

The Growth Management Act is a multi-layered piece of legislation. It includes an overall framework for managing goals as well as a number of "must do" items. In order to assure a good deal of room for local control and local conditions the act also provides for a good deal of conversation meant to guide locales as they plan.

Achieving the goals of the GMA has proven to be, "A tough nut to crack" because the GMA provides local jurisdictions with a good deal of digression in how goals are to be achieved, assumes to a high degree that a jurisdiction is correct in its approach to managing growth, and lacks specific language in some important areas.

The GMA provides a good deal of opportunity for jurisdictions diligently trying to manage growth for the benefit of all citizens to do just that. GMA is also susceptible to manipulation by interest groups and others seeking to achieve this or that agenda.

Because growth management is something that plays out over decades rather than months or years, it will be some time yet before we are able to actually measure the success of the act in achieving its stated goals.

A Framework For Planning

As explained in Washington's Administrative Code regarding the Growth Management Act:

"WAC 365-196-010 Background.

Through the Growth Management Act, the legislature provided a new framework for land use planning and the regulation of development in Washington state. The act was enacted in response to problems associated with uncoordinated and unplanned growth and a lack of common goals in the conservation and the wise use of our lands. Perceived problems included increased traffic congestion, pollution, school overcrowding, urban sprawl, and the loss of rural lands.

(1) Major features of the Act's framework include:

> (a) A requirement that counties with specified populations and rates of growth and the cities within them adopt comprehensive plans and development regulations under the act. Other counties can choose to be covered by this requirement, thereby including the cities they contain.

> (b) A set of common goals to guide the development of comprehensive plans and development regulations.

> (c) The concept that the process should be a "bottom up" effort, involving early and continuous public participation, with the central locus of decision-making at the local level, bounded by the goals and requirements of the act.

> (d) Requirements for the locally developed plans to be internally consistent, consistent with county-wide planning policies and multicounty planning policies, and consistent with the plans of other counties and cities where there are common borders or related regional issues.

(e) A requirement that development regulations adopted to implement the comprehensive plans be consistent with such plans.

(f) The principle that development and the providing of public facilities and services needed to support development should occur concurrently.

(g) A determination that planning and plan implementation actions should address difficult issues that have resisted resolution in the past, such as:

>(i) The timely financing of needed infrastructure;

>(ii) Providing adequate and affordable housing for all economic segments of the population;

>(iii) Concentrating growth in urban areas, provided with adequate urban services;

>(iv) The siting of essential public facilities;

>(v) The designation and conservation of agricultural, forest, and mineral resource lands;

>(vi) The designation and protection of environmentally critical areas.

(h) A determination that comprehensive planning can simultaneously address these multiple issues by focusing on the land development process as a common underlying factor.

(i) An intention that economic development be encouraged and fostered within the planning and regulatory scheme established for managing growth.

(j) A recognition that the act is a fundamental building block of regulatory reform. The state and local government have invested considerable resources in an act that should serve as the integrating framework for other land use related laws.

(k) A desire to recognize the importance of rural areas and provide for rural economic development.

(l) A requirement that counties and cities must periodically review and update their comprehensive plans and development regulations to ensure continued compliance with the goals and requirements of the act.

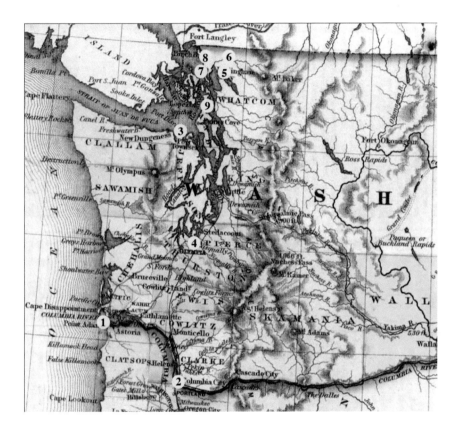

Three Fundamentals

1. County-wide Planning Policies are developed to assure consistency between city and county plans.
2. Comprehensive Plans based on the framework provided by County-wide Planning Policies are developed by the county and each of its cities. The Comprehensive Plans detail how GMA goals are to be achieved.
3. Development Regulations implementing the comprehensive plans are adopted.

The regulations, plans and, policies must all be internally consistent and, externally consistent with each other.

Planning To Accommodate Growth Is A "Bottom Up" Effort

The GMA imposes requirements on cities and counties but, to a large extent, allows local jurisdictions to decide how to fulfill those requirements in any way they choose so long as the requirements are met.

RCW 36.70A.3201 provides legislative intent regarding the place local planning has in accommodating growth under the GMA:

1. When challenged, boards (and courts) are to apply a "…more deferential standard of review to actions of counties and cities…" than the more usual "preponderance of evidence standard;"
2. Counties are given a "…broad range of discretion…" in deciding how to comply with the law;
3. While local planning must "…take place within a framework of state goals and requirements…" the responsibility for planning and harmonizing the requirements of the law with local plans and implementing those plans "rests with" the local community.

In communities as is the case with individuals, freedom and responsibility are inextricably linked. While the GMA placed fetters on cities and counties capable of curbing the most blatant excesses of both, the extreme deference given the decisions of cities and counties in planning has also politicized the planning process to a great extent. Special interest groups with large sums of money at their disposal and intimate connections to decision makers at the state level have found it more and more possible to control the planning process as the GMA matures.

Public Participation

The term "public participation" is one of the most used terms in the GMA. Throughout the act, most notably **RCW 36.70A.140**, the need for public participation is noted and required.

Counties and Cities must:

1. Establish and broadly disseminate to the public a public participation program that;
2. Clearly identifies procedures providing for early and continuous public participation in the development and amendment of comprehensive plans and development regulations.

The procedures set forward must:

1. Provide for broad dissemination of proposals and alternatives available;
2. Provide opportunity for written comments;
3. Provide for public meetings after effective notice;
4. Establish opportunities for open discussion;
5. Make provision for open discussion, communication programs and information services and;
6. Demonstrate there has been consideration of and response to public comments.

The extensive public participation requirements required of cities and counties by the GMA is a vital offset to the politicization almost assured by other aspects of the act.

Countywide Planning Policies – The Local "Framework"

The GMA creates a tension between cities and counties planning under the act.

1. Counties determine population and employment targets and then assign targets the cities of the county must meet;
2. But the cities of the county decide how to meet their assigned targets;
3. The act recognizes that counties are regional governments and must plan regionally;
4. The act recognizes that cities are "primary providers of urban governmental services within urban growth areas;
5. City and County Comprehensive plans must, nevertheless, be consistent with one another despite sometimes conflicting objectives.

To create the common ground needed to assure consistency between the plans adopted by jurisdictions with sometimes conflicting purposes and needs, cities and counties are required to adopt, working together, Countywide Planning Policies (**RCW 36.70A.210**) governing the plans and development regulations of both entities. While most aspects of planning can be challenged by regular citizens, Countywide Planning Policies (often called CWPP) may only be challenged by cities or the governor to the growth management hearings board.

Countywide Planning Policies are:

1. Written statements of policy agreed upon in advance of the planning process;

2. The agreed upon policies provide the "countywide framework from which county and city comprehensive plans are developed and adopted;"
3. Do not alter the land-use powers of cities.

One of the tensions created by GMA comes from the fact that counties assign growth that cities are required to plan for yet cities have the choice to accommodate growth in ways that may not be approved of by the county.

Comprehensive Plans Must Be Developed And Adopted

Counties and cities are required to create and adopt meaningful comprehensive plans **RCW 36.70A.040.** Comprehensive plans must:

1. Include a map, or maps illustrating zoning, boundaries and, infrastructure plans;
2. Include descriptive text "…covering objectives, principles, and standards used to develop the comprehensive plan;
3. Be internally consistent documents;
4. And all elements of the plan "…shall be consistent with the future land use map."

Each comprehensive plan must include:

1. A land use element;
2. A housing element;
3. A capital facilities plan element;
4. A utilities element;
5. A rural element;
6. A transportation element;
7. An economic development element
8. A park and recreation element (in most cases)

Cities and counties are also allowed to include a number of optional elements to their comprehensive plans if they wish but each of those elements must maintain the internal consistency required of the entire plan.

Counties, their cities and, citizens alike have experienced difficulty dealing with the fact that comprehensive plans pre-growth management and comprehensive plans post-growth management perform significantly different functions. Before the GMA changed everything, comprehensive plans along with the goals and policies they contain were a bit like political wish lists. A planner, asked by a mayor regarding a comprehensive plan, "What does that mean?" might respond as the punch line of an old joke has it, "Anything you want it to mean." Under the GMA, goals put forward in comprehensive plans retain that kind of nebulous lack of any real meaning but the policies put forward in a comprehensive plan as compliant with countywide planning policies are directive; they require actions called out by the policies.

Comprehensive Plans Must Accommodate/Enable Future Growth

RCW 36.70A.115 requires Counties and cities to "ensure" that comprehensive plans and/or development regulations provide enough land, properly zoned, to accommodate allocated housing and employment growth. Sufficient land includes the land needed for new roads and other infrastructure, schools, parks and all the other kinds of land needed to accommodate growth.

The Washington GMA is based on a carrot rather than stick approach. The purpose of the act is to make UGAs attractive to new citizens; so attractive that most make the free choice to live in an urban rather than a rural environment.

An issue that has developed over time with growth management is that cities routinely look for ways to avoid actually enabling land supplies to accept growth projected for the future. Rather than making the city's land supply easily accessible and so attractive people want to live there the effort has gone the other way; make the city expensive and difficult to develop in so less development occurs in the city. Some of the more interesting strategies developed to shift projected growth include:

1. **"Zoning" Urban Growth Areas to accept large amounts of growth but as policy, prohibiting growth until annexation takes place, while refusing annexation during the 20-year planning horizon;**
2. **In theory, all the growth projected for a city can be accommodated in a single building if an assumption is made that the building will be tall enough to contain enough apartments and office space to accept that growth. Some cities have adopted a slightly less obvious approach assuming density exceeding that**

seen in downtown Seattle or Bellevue will take place even in small cities.

3. Extraordinarily difficult and lengthy permitting processes designed to make building so expensive developers decline to develop.

4. Land supplies that do not match market demand to assure new residents will reject the options available to them and choose to live elsewhere.

To work, growth management planning must be realistic.

This is a model of what must occur on just one jurisdiction over a 20 year period (2002 – 2022) based on that jurisdiction's plan for itself. Yellow represents existing landmark buildings in the town, magenta represents what has actually been built, and the remaining colors represent a mix of commercial, residential, governmental, and other buildings planned for the town's central core.

Development Regulations Must Implement Comprehensive Plans

Development regulations are "…the controls placed on development or land use activities by a county or city."

Prior to the GMA, development regulations a city or county had in place were the controlling regulations governing the jurisdiction. If a conflict existed between the comprehensive plan and the development regulation the regulation ruled.

The GMA changed all that in fundamental ways in that GMA required jurisdictions to develop comprehensive plans and then adopt development regulations consistent with the comprehensive plan; the horse was placed before the cart.

The change was significant enough to convince the legislature to extend the consistency requirement to all counties and cities in the state. As of 1992 even those jurisdictions not required to plan under GMA are still required to have comprehensive plans and development regulations in a state of consistency with one another.

The requirement that comprehensive plans and the development regulations implementing them be both internally consistent as well as consistent with one another was a huge change. The change brought the comprehensive plan process to the fore in citizen's minds. Because comprehensive plans are more susceptible to citizen input (development regulations seem to most people to be more of a legalistic process) the prioritization of the comprehensive plan meant citizens engaging in the comprehensive process were actually having an influence on the future shape of their communities rather than simply working on a wish list that could be ignored later by writing implementing rules inconsistent with the comprehensive plans the rules were meant to deal with.

Four Kinds Of Land Must Be Identified For GMA To Work

GMA establishes three important land supplies and one type of land to protect if long term planning for growth is to work:

1. Resource lands are to be set aside and protected. Three types of resource lands are called out; Agricultural, Forest, and Mineral;
2. Urban lands in the form of Urban Growth Areas are to be provided for with sufficient land available to accommodate projected growth in a way that attracts residents to settle inside the growth areas;
3. Rural lands are set aside to allow those desiring to live a traditional rural lifestyle to have that choice and;
4. Critical Areas are to be delineated and preserved.

Note that "Rural" lands and "Agricultural" lands are not the same. Agricultural resource lands are lands set aside to be preserved and to support commercial agriculture. "Rural lands are set aside to support that portion of the population desiring to choose a traditional rural lifestyle. Confusion between the two accounts for a good deal of tension as comprehensive planning is done by cities and counties.

Resource Lands (Ag., Forestry, Mineral) Are To Be Set Aside And Managed To Ensure The Long Term Health And Survival Of The Industry They Support

Resource lands are among the most protected lands required to be established and conserved by the GMA.

RCW 36.70A.040 requires that counties and their cities "shall designate" lands to be utilized for the three uses and that the jurisdictions shall "…adopt development regulations conserving…" the designated lands.

RCW 36.70A.060 requires that regulations adopted to govern the use of "…lands adjacent to agricultural, forest, or mineral resource lands shall not interfere with the continued use, in the accustomed manner and in accordance with best management practices, of these designated lands for the production of food, agricultural products, or timber, or for the extraction of minerals.

A combination of Washington State Supreme Court decisions as well as Growth Management Hearings Board decisions has solidified the GMA's intention that lands designated for agriculture, forestry, and mineral uses may not be converted to other uses without extensive process.

It's an oddity that over the years the perceptions of both decision makers and the public at large has elevated agriculture to the top of the resource lands triad but the fact remains, each of the three resource land supplies are to be vigorously protected from intrusion by uses not compatible with them.

Forest Lands Are To Be Utilized To Assure The Forest Products Industry Continues To Survive And Thrive In Washington

Forest lands are not playgrounds although they can be utilized for recreation but only if the use does not impact their ability to support and enhance the economic health of the forest products industry.

Agricultural Lands Are To Be Utilized To Assure Commercial Agriculture Continues To Survive And Thrive In Washington

Agricultural lands are not set aside to provide for lovely views enhancing bucolic images of days gone by for Sunday drives or bicycle rides. They are set aside to provide for commercial agriculture, a sometimes messy, stinky, loud economic sector.

Mineral Resource Lands Are Set Aside To Assure The Minerals, Especially Sand And Gravel Needed In A Healthy Economy, Can Be Provided

Urban Development Depends on Mineral Resource Lands

Rural Lands Are To Be Set Aside And Managed To Achieve GMA Goals

Rural lands are, based on the GMA, one of the most important land supplies cities and counties must provide. They are also one of the most disliked land supplies so far as many activist groups are concerned.

An important distinction that is almost always overlooked; rural lands are *not* designated agricultural lands. Rural land serve a different purpose than designated Ag lands.

Rural lands are so important that the legislature, in 2002, added findings about them meant to clarify what rural lands are all about. According to **RCW 36.70A.011:** "The legislature finds that this chapter is intended to recognize the importance of rural lands and rural character to Washington's economy, its people, and its environment, while respecting regional differences."

Rural lands are to be managed by counties to foster land use patterns and develop a local vision of rural character that will:

1. Help preserve rural based economies;
2. Help preserve traditional rural lifestyles;
3. Encourage economic prosperity for rural residents;
4. Provide for opportunities for small scale rural based employment as well as self-employment;
5. Allow the operation of rural based agricultural, commercial, recreational, and tourist businesses that are consistent with existing and planned land use patterns;
6. Provide for compatibility with use of the land for fish and wildlife habitat;
7. Foster private stewardship of the land as well as preservation of open space and;

8. Enhance the rural sense of community and quality of life.

Critical Areas Must Be Delineated, Protected, And Preserved

Rural Land Must Be Provided For As Outlined In A County's Comprehensive Plan

RCW 36.70A.070 requires counties include a rural element in their Comprehensive Plans.

The Rural Element includes lands the GMA applies to that are not designated for urban growth, agriculture, forest, or mineral resources.

The Rural Element:

1. Must permit rural development;
2. Must allow forestry and agriculture;
3. Must provide for a variety of rural densities and uses and;
4. Must allow the essential public facilities and rural governmental services requires to provide for permitted densities and uses.

To achieve a variety of rural densities and uses counties are allowed to provide for:

1. Clustering;
2. Density transfers;
3. Design guidelines;
4. Conservation easements;
5. Other innovative techniques.

An early Growth Management Hearings Board member characterized lands zoned Rural in Washington's GMA counties as being "The leftover meatloaf in the Growth Management refrigerator." The board, nevertheless, pointed out that under GMA rural lands serve an important function.

The "new" (now over a decade old) legislative findings of 2002 emphasize the importance of rural lands in preserving traditional rural lifestyles and rural character.

Many activist groups want to, and have been successful in, dramatically restricting the appropriate use of rural lands in Washington's counties.

The effort to preserve rural character and rural lifestyles is likely to take a front and center position in discussions about the GMA in coming years. Through the first quarter century of growth management in Washington the use and, therefore, function of the state's rural lands have been severely restricted with the rural economy and quality of life suffering as a result. The next ten years may determine the entire fate of the rural lands and rural economy for decades to come.

Attracting Growth To Urban Growth Areas (UGA)

The concept of Urban Growth Areas (UGAs) is fundamental to the GMA's approach to managing growth.

RCW 36.70A.110 requires that counties planning under GMA designate Urban Growth Areas (UGAs) inside of which urban growth must be encouraged and outside of which only growth "not urban in nature," is to be allowed.

UGAs are defined as:

1. All the land inside the city limits of the incorporated cities of a county;
2. Plus additional, unincorporated, lands, if needed to capture growth, adjacent to city boundaries and selected for inclusion in the UGA through the comprehensive planning process;

UGAs are created to capture as much of the growth taking place in a county as possible. Problems arise when a city or cities required to absorb growth chooses to turn its back on growth. If UGAs do not capture growth assigned to them by the county, then growth is shifted to areas the GMA was created to reduce growth in.

Urban Areas Are To Be Identified And Managed To Achieve GMA Goals

Projected Land Supply Needs Must Be Determined Using A Supply And Demand Analysis

RCW 36.70A.115 requires that comprehensive plans and development regulations "…must provide sufficient land capacity for development," so that allocated housing and employment growth can be accommodated.

A 2009 amendment to the GMA was intended to assure cities and counties not only provided the land supply necessary for homes but also to assure the land supplies necessary to support the populations housed on those homes was available.

Necessary land supplies that must be identified in the development of comprehensive plans and development regulations include:

1. Medical;
2. Governmental;
3. Institutional;
4. Commercial;
5. Service;
6. Retail;
7. Other nonresidential uses.

Additionally, county-wide planning policies are to include consideration of future development of commercial and industrial facilities.

Almost immediately on adoption of the GMA, activist groups, business organizations, and other interested parties were working to use the act to achieve their own goals; each group thought the act had been passed just for their benefit.

One almost universally utilized way to frustrate the GMA's requirement for a 20 year land supply to accommodate population and economic growth was to manipulate the alleged land supply in a UGA to provide the appearance of adequacy but not the reality.

 The requirement that adequate supplies for all the major land use needs a population must have to function as a community requires more than a cursory look at land supply.

As is the case with many GMA issues, enforcing the requirements is an ongoing issue.

Adequate land supplies for future commercial, institutional, and industrial needs are to be provided for in large cities and in small cities.

Concurrency Goes Hand In Hand With An Adequate Land Supply

Concurrency is a state in which adequate public facilities, services, and/or strategies to provide those facilities and services are in place at the time a development is ready to occupy.

The adequate land supply required by the GMA is of no consequence if that supply cannot be utilized to actually accommodate population growth.

The GMA only specifically addresses concurrency in relation to transportation funding but, the courts and the hearings boards have found other concurrency requirements are either specifically or intuitively required of a city and county by the GMA as well as by other statutes supporting the GMA. Most specifically, goal 12 of the GMA is the only goal with an imperative; "Ensure that those public facilities and services necessary to support development shall be adequate to serve..."

Concurrency requirements in the GMA and other statutes were meant to assure growth assigned to cities and counties could be accommodated during the 20 year planning period required by GMA.

All too often, counties and, especially, cities, have used concurrency to stall or stop growth rather than to assure growth as the GMA requires.

Concurrency Must Be Provided For Within The Planning Period

Many Hearings Board decisions address an overlooked aspect of concurrency; concurrency is supposed to be provided for within the planning timeframe a comprehensive plan addresses.

Cities and Counties can phase development throughout the 20 year period but, as Boards have warned, designated UGAs especially must be available for growth during the planning period they were established to serve. The time does not reset with any of the periodic updates.

The Western Hearings Board summed the issue up and reflected the tenor of other Board decisions saying, in relation to a case regarding the City of Oak Harbor:

"Concurrency requires adopted level of service standards, a projection of future needs, a financially feasible capital facilities financing plan that meets those needs, and the assurance that the facilities will be in place within a specified time frame."

Jurisdictions Must Consider Concurrency As An On-Going Requirement

RCW 36.70A.120 deals with planning activities and capital budget decisions requiring that counties and cities "...shall perform its activities and make capital budget decisions in conformity with its comprehensive plan."

Perhaps more than any other aspect of the GMA, cities and counties have played fast and loose with capital facilities and concurrency. Concurrency is widely used to restrict the development necessary to support assigned growth, especially in the areas designed to capture growth, the UGAs.

Equally ignored is the absolute obligation cities especially, but counties as well, to have the infrastructure required to support growth within the 20 year planning period a UGA is sized to support.

A likely difficulty cities and counties will face in coming years is that their respective neglect of the requirement that concurrency be achieved within the planning period will lay a huge financial obligation on the jurisdictions who've ignored the requirement for a decade and a half and more.

Urban Growth Areas provided with utilities and other infrastructure in a timely manner provide land that can be built to modern urban standards, thus diverting growth from areas outside the growth areas:

Lands unsupplied with urban services, even if located in an urban growth area, cannot serve the purpose they are intended for and, thus, disable the mechanisms meant to manage growth.

Here, land planned for as many as 12 housing units to the acre as well as some commercial services has gone unserved for 17 years of the 20 year planning period it was to provide for.

The GMA Requires Accommodation Of Growth, Internal Consistency, And Implementation

The GMA was enacted to bring about intentional change. As explained in **WAC 365-196-010**, "In many areas, the pattern called for in the act is a departure from the pattern that existed prior to the act. As a consequence, areas developed prior to the act may not clearly fit into the pattern of development established in the act."

In addition to accommodation of growth and internal consistency **RCW 36.70A.120** requires follow through; planning counties and cities "shall perform" activities and "make capital budget decisions in conformity with its comprehensive plan."

Many cities and counties appear to have largely ignored the GMA requirement that each make capital facility decisions based on comprehensive plans. This is an area where jurisdiction's feet have not been held to the fire but, as Urban Growth Areas originally established in the mid to late 1990s reach their maturity, the need to assure growth projected for those UGAs can take place may take front and center stage in discussions regarding growth management.

The problem is the time and expense required to hold a jurisdiction accountable. Most jurisdictions know that they can take nearly any action they want and nobody will spend the money and take the time to require the jurisdiction to plan and implement their plans in accordance with the law. Contentious cases can easily take 5 years and many, many thousands of dollars to resolve from Hearings Board to high court.

What Does All This Mean To You?

WAC 365-196-010 points to a number of "major features of the act's framework" commenting that achieving the legislature's wish for coordinated and planned growth replace the uncoordinated and unplanned growth seen as rampant in 1990 is based on "A determination that comprehensive planning can simultaneously address these multiple issues by focusing on the land development process as a common underlying factor."

This means the GMA is the paramount way in which the State of Washington addresses legislative goals aimed at environmental enhancement, economic prosperity, and quality of life for all citizens.

So What Are We Supposed To Do As We Plan Under GMA?

We are to:

1. Think realistically about how we can all work best in community to achieve the 14 goals for our community contained in the GMA while we accommodate population growth expected in coming years and;
2. Develop plans that allow us to achieve those statewide goals locally in ways that are consistent with local aspirations so far as is possible.

Most Important Of All

The GMA is about providing appropriate lifestyle choices in ways that encourage citizens to act in appropriate ways; It is not about restricting choice in ways that degrade quality of life, the economy, and the environment as citizens rebel against having lifestyles imposed on them.

ISSUES AND POTENTIAL SOLUTIONS

THE PROBLEM WITH GROWTH PROJECTIONS

Originally only a single growth projection was offered counties. Because the projection was the official estimate of likely population, counties were expected to base their plans on that estimate demonstrating with data why a deviation from the estimate was being considered.

Early on, the legislature required OFM to establish a likely population estimate accompanied by "a reasonable range" high and low projection. The OFM "middle" range projection is defined as "the most likely to occur." The "mid" range projection may or may not be near the midpoint between high and low. The "most likely to occur" projection is determined by data. High and low projections are described by OFM as representing "bands of uncertainty."

Allowing a range of projections allows the selection of a population projection to address 20 years of growth to be more politically charged than a simple process based on data ought to be. Counties wanting to reject growth can, and do, project low growth numbers for political rather than science based reasons. The counties then justify knowingly under-projecting likely growth by simply stating that the projection selected was "in the range," provided and was, thus, compliant with GMA.

In effect, the population "range" approach has meant a return to pre-GMA days in which jurisdictions say, once again, "We'll take the 'good' growth and we'll do all we can to make sure you get the 'bad' growth.

A SIMPLE SOLUTION

Currently, the GMA is unclear on the issue of population projections. A simple adjustment to the law could require counties to base the projection they plan for on the most likely projection provided by OFM and then allow solid, data based, deviation within the range but *only* when the work used to justify deviation is clearly shown and explained as to the reason for the deviation.

THE CONCURRENCY PROBLEM

While Hearings Board decisions have been pretty clear about requirements that Urban Growth Areas are to be ready to accept growth within the 20-year period they were established to serve, cities and counties routinely ignore the requirement.

As a result of the neglect, many urban growth areas are the most protected *from* growth regions in their respective counties.

The result?

Many of the state's cities are not achieving the share of growth assigned them, not because new populations don't want to live in an urban setting but, rather, because the cities are effectively rejecting population growth, one of the problems the Growth Management Act was designed to correct.

Three areas of the concurrency requirement need to be addressed. Two deal with timing while the third has to do with scope.

First, because cities and counties have neglected, for decades, to provide the infrastructure needed inside of growth areas, those same cities and counties now face a near insurmountable obstacle; very large portions of the infrastructure those jurisdictions should have already planned for, financed, and built, has not been either financed or built.

Workable solutions to the mess cause by jurisdictions flaunting of the law are difficult to come by because they were supposed to be phased over 20 years but, at the very least, legislators, and others, desiring a workable growth management effort ought to be asking questions like:

1. Under RCW 36.70A.106, specifically the department now known as the Department of Commerce, and all other State Departments have been responsible for reviewing plan and regulation changes by helping cities and counties with growth management issues for nearly a quarter of a century. The oversight has been seriously lacking. Why has the State, via this required review and comment by State Departments not been more proactive in assuring jurisdictions are not only planning for concurrency but actually achieving concurrency?
2. Hearings Board decisions have made it clear that cities and counties must provide for concurrency within the timeframe required by law with no excuses. Jurisdictions out of compliance with the law lose the ability to apply for and acquire certain kinds of grant money. Should jurisdictions unable to provide for concurrency within the planning period be automatically declared to be out of compliance?
3. This is a statewide problem. Why hasn't legislature clarified the law?

Although there is no simple solution to this very big problem, an initial step would be to revise the language in RCW 36.70A.106 to specifically require the Department of Commerce to review proposed plan updates for adequate capital facility planning and funding plans. The Department should also have the capability of finding a County or City out of compliance if there is not adequate planning in the proposed planning documents.

It might also prove to be beneficial were the law to be amended to specifically mention infrastructure needs other than transportation (sewer, water, transit, etc.) as requiring concurrency.

Challenging City Or County Actions Under GMA

Shortly after the passage of the initial GMA, a second round of legislation established a quasi-judicial process allowing those impacted by the passage of plans and development regulations governed by the GMA to challenge the plans and regulations before a Growth Management Hearings Board.

The Hearings Boards are not courts, they are boards authorized by the legislature "...to "hear and determine" allegations a city, county, or state agency has not complied with the goals and requirements of the GMA, related provisions of the Shoreline Management Act (SMA), RCW 90.58, and the State Environmental Policy Act (SEPA), RCW 43.21C."

Hearings Board members are not elected, they are political appointees.

Citizens are allowed to file with the Boards "Petitions For Review" *pro se* or, without representation by an attorney.

The ability to challenge the actions of local government *pro se* has been an important power granted to those regulated under the GMA by the actions of local jurisdictions. Challenges put forward with legal representation can cost tens, or even hundreds, of thousands of dollars. The ability to challenge *pro se* has allowed for the resolution of numerous growth management issues that would not have been addressed absent that right.

Hearings Board decisions are appealable to the courts; in fact, Hearings Board decisions have been overturned many times by the courts during the quarter century since the initial passage of the GMA.

Unfortunately even a challenge filed *pro se* cannot be appealed to even local Superior Courts without substantial expense. Citizen involvement in the judicial process breaks down at the Court level.

A Simple Solution

An easy and relatively inexpensive change in the law could require court review of Hearings Board decisions argued *pro se* on request of the petitioner. The Hearings Boards would have to provide a transcript of the Hearings Board proceedings to the Superior Court Judge doing the review along with one copy of the evidence presented. Each "side" in the case would be allowed a few pages of briefing regarding the issues. The reviewing judge would then have the option to overturn or confirm the Hearings Board. Appeals to higher courts would be handled as they are today.

The ability to have a fully qualified judge review a Hearings Board decision would provide significant advantages as jurisdictions shape their planning efforts under growth management. At present, many aspects of the act that should be explored in the legal venue are not because going to court is an extremely expensive proposition. Well funded activist groups as well as jurisdictions not having to worry about expense have taken advantage of the situation by passing questionable legislation then daring anyone to go through the time and expense of a challenge. Access to an appeal with meaningful review of a politically appointed body's decisions about important aspects of growth management could make for significantly better understanding of what the law is and what it actually compels.

Both Jack and Clayton would like to thank you for purchasing this book. We hope you have found it informative and useful. As stated at the beginning, this book is a brief and informational introduction to what is often referred to as simply the "GMA"

We encourage those wishing for a more exhaustive, technical document to read the "Short Course on Local Planning Resource Guide" and to attend some of the events the Washington State Department of Commerce has. Everything can be found at the State site located here: http://www.commerce.wa.gov/Services/localgovernment/ GrowthManagement/Short-Course-on-Local-Planning/Pages/default.aspx

The Washington State Growth Management Act: Plain and Simple, was written because the authors have found, after nearly a quarter century of work on Growth Management issues, that even fairly informed and involved people have trouble keeping up with and understanding the issues surrounding Washington's GMA.

Over that same quarter century Jack and Clayton have written on GMA issues for the Journal of the American Planning Association, presented to both attorneys and Growth Management Hearings Board members as part of Law Seminars International's continuing education program for attorneys, written an exhaustive, peer reviewed, case study analysis of the impacts of the GMA on Whatcom County, Washington for the American Planning Association's publication Practicing Planner, provided Op-Eds for newspapers, produced white papers on the GMA for the Washington Association of Realtors, and have presented on numerous occasions to realty and building association audiences.

Last, Clayton Petree and his father Jack own Public Policy Perspectives in Bellingham, Washington. Both are dedicated to exploring practical approaches to environmental issues businesses can adopt to be both environmentally sensitive and profitable. The two have written more than 2,500 articles for regional, national and international publications.

You can reach Jack and Clayton via e-mail at:
publicpolicyperspectives@comcast.net

39894725R00043

Made in the USA
Lexington, KY
16 March 2015